To, Luan with love

From: Yvonne S.

God's blessings and best wishes
to you and your family.

Jan. 2016

Hang In There

Blue Mountain Arts®

New and Best-Selling Titles

By Susan Polis Schutz:
To My Daughter with Love on the Important Things in Life
To My Son with Love

By Douglas Pagels:
For You, My Soul Mate
100 Things to Always Remember... and One Thing to Never Forget
Required Reading for All Teenagers

By Marci:
Friends Are Forever
10 Simple Things to Remember
To My Daughter
You Are My "Once in a Lifetime"

By Wally Amos, with Stu Glauberman:
The Path to Success Is Paved with Positive Thinking

By M. Butler and D. Mastromarino:
Take Time for You

By James Downton, Jr.:
Today, I Will... Words to Inspire Positive Life Changes

By Donna Fargo:
I Thanked God for You Today

Anthologies:
A Daughter Is Life's Greatest Gift
A Sister's Love Is Forever
A Son Is Life's Greatest Gift
Dream Big, Stay Positive, and Believe in Yourself
Friends for Life
God Is Always Watching Over You
Hang In There
Keep Believing in Yourself and Your Dreams
The Love Between a Mother and Daughter Is Forever
The Strength of Women
Think Positive Thoughts Every Day
Words Every Woman Should Remember

Hang In There

Life Can Be Hard Sometimes, but It's Going to Be Okay

Edited by
Patricia Wayant

Blue Mountain Press™
Boulder, Colorado

We wish to thank Susan Polis Schutz for permission to reprint the following poems that appear in this publication: "You Can Handle Any Problems That Life Brings," "Tomorrow Is a New Day," "Just Do Your Best," and "Dreams can come true...." Copyright © 1983, 1986, 1988 by Stephen Schutz and Susan Polis Schutz. All rights reserved.

Library of Congress Control Number: 2011944849
ISBN: 978-1-59842-639-7

N and Blue Mountain Press are registered in U.S. Patent and Trademark Office.
Certain trademarks are used under license.

Printed in China.
Second Printing: 2012

⊕ This book is printed on recycled paper.

This book is printed on paper that has been specially produced to be acid free (neutral pH) and contains no groundwood or unbleached pulp. It conforms with the requirements of the American National Standards Institute, Inc., so as to ensure that this book will last and be enjoyed by future generations.

Blue Mountain Arts, Inc.

P.O. Box 4549, Boulder, Colorado 80306

Contents

7 Donna Fargo

8 Terry Bairnson

11 Jason Blume

12 Brian Gill

15 Julie Rojics

16 Donna Fargo

18 Jason Blume

20 Judith Mammay

22 Paula Michele Adams

24 Douglas Pagels

27 Suzy Toronto

28 Douglas Pagels

31 Susan Polis Schutz

32 Alin Austin

34 Pamela Owens Renfro

36 Caroline Comerford

38 Bonnie St. John

40 Douglas Pagels

43 Susan Polis Schutz

44 Lamisha Serf

47 Linda Sackett-Morrison

48 Donna Fargo

50 Paula Finn

52 Lisa Mae Huddleston

55 Ashley Rice

56 Susan Polis Schutz

59 Donna Fargo

60 Linda E. Knight

63 Marion Wilson

64 Author Unknown

65 Author Unknown

65 Victor Hugo

67 Susan Polis Schutz

68 Donna Fargo

70 Candy Paull

72 Rachel Snyder

75 Jason Blume

76 Lamisha Serf

78 Maria Mullins

80 Nancye Sims

83 Rachel Snyder

84 Nancye Sims

86 Douglas Pagels

88 Linda E. Knight

91 Douglas Pagels

92 Acknowledgments

Life Can Be Hard Sometimes

Life is full of surprises — some good and some not so good. When your world has been turned upside down, remember... just as there are clearer skies and brighter days after a hard rain, the stormy weather in your life will also change. Life hurts sometimes, but you're a survivor and you will make the best of the situation. You will find positive ways to handle disappointment, you will learn valuable lessons, and you will discover strengths to empower you. Life has its seasons, but seasons change, and you will get through this.

~ Donna Fargo

It's Going to Be Okay

There will be times when you're going to need so much courage. There will be times... when you'll feel like crying yourself to sleep. When your confidence is shaken. When you're scared, angry, and confused. When you can't believe this is happening to you.

But for every one of those situations, there will also be times when you look deep inside and realize... you're going to be okay.

There will be times when you find out that you're such a fighter. When you discover how strong you really can be and that you're truly a survivor.

The people with the biggest hearts are the ones who can be most vulnerable sometimes. But they're also the ones who have the capacity to hold on tight and find a way through.

You're one of those people.

~ Terry Bairnson

They Say
Hard Times
Make Us Stronger

The challenges you face
will bring you lessons
and change you in positive ways
    you never imagined.
You will find that you are stronger
    than you ever knew.
You will learn that you are loved
    and cared for
and things can turn out okay —
even when it seems impossible.
You will find that even
    the hardest times pass.

~ Jason Blume

Just Hold On and Keep Your Spirits Up

Never forget what a treasure you are ➤ Try to realize how important you are in the eyes of the world ➤ No matter where you go, hopes and hearts travel beside you every step of the way ➤ Even though difficulties come to everyone, it isn't fair when they hang around longer than they should ➤ But until a new day comes along, trust that you'll always be strong enough to see things through ➤ Remember how much strength and courage you have inside ➤ You can find all the patience it takes ➤

You can turn to the times in the past when
challenges were met, when you survived, when
you were rewarded with success, and when you
learned to believe in so much within you ⌒ You
have so much going for you, and you're going
to see your way through anything that comes
along ⌒ Brighter days are going to find a way
to shine in your windows and chase away any
blues ⌒ Because no one deserves more smiles,
success, friendship, or love ...than you ⌒

~ Brian Gill

You Can Accomplish Anything You Put Your Mind To

Inner strength, determination,
    and courage aren't just words...
        they are part of who you are.
Look within yourself,
    and you will find the strength
        to rise to any challenge.

Know that even the smallest step forward
    is important
and brings you closer to your goals.
It may be hard, but nothing comes easily.
Remember that beyond the clouds
    is the brilliant blue of the sky.

Life's finest moments will come
    after you've weathered the storm.
If you believe,
    anything is possible.
        ~ Julie Rojics

Ten Golden Rules
for a Better Life

1. Live your life with purpose; don't just do "whatever," or "whatever" might just be what you get.

2. Develop a compassionate spirit and a loving heart; you will feel better about yourself, and others will feel better about you.

3. Be honest and guard your integrity no matter what the rest of the world is doing; they're not the ones who have to live with you — you are.

4. Believe in yourself and always do what's right; a clear conscience will keep you on the right path.

5. Be as good as your word and don't make promises you're not going to keep.

6. Be fair to others, especially those less fortunate; there may come a time you have to walk in their shoes.

7. Keep a positive attitude and speak encouraging words; you'll hear them rise up in you when you need them, and others will remember them when they need lifting up.

8. Don't take your natural talents for granted; use them to nourish your soul and to touch lives, and they will be multiplied.

9. When you feel discouraged or unlucky, remember the times you've been fortunate, and that knowledge will help balance out your fears.

10. Remember that what you do today will show up tomorrow, so when you make important decisions, think about tomorrow today.

~ Donna Fargo

Courage is not
the absence of fear;
it is feeling our fears —
and facing them anyway.

The challenges you're facing are not easy.
But one step at a time,
you will get through them —
because you are strong,
resilient, and powerful,
and you have the love and support
of people who will stand beside you.

You are a courageous person.
You've come through hard times before,
and you'll come through this too.

You are stronger than you know.

~ Jason Blume

But Why Me?

Sometimes we are overwhelmed with
the obstacles we are given in our lives,
and we ask "Why me?"
And often, when the answers elude us,
we believe that the trials through which
we suffer are unfair and harsh.
But there are answers,
even though we may not recognize them.
In this world, we are all connected
and there is a reason for whatever happens.
We must remain strong in the face of adversity
and meet the challenges one day at a time.

And as time heals us,
both body and soul,
we may come to understand
the meaning of our trials
and recognize the good
that came from them.
We may take pride in knowing that
we made it through them
and as a result are much stronger
than we were before.

~ Judith Mammay

Life Is What You Make It

Life has a way of throwing us off course,
surprising us into making changes
we weren't planning on making.
Things may get difficult,
and you may struggle to do what's right.
But each new day brings new hope
and offers us a new chance to get it right.

Don't focus on what was.
Look forward to what can be,
and then do all you can to make it a reality.

Life is what you make of it,
and the challenges that come your way
are opportunities to right what is wrong.
Don't get discouraged, and don't give up.
You have it all inside yourself,
and you can overcome anything
if you put your mind to it.

~ Paula Michele Adams

Sometimes You Just Need to Start Over

When it's time for a new beginning...
You need faith. That things will be better.
You need strength.
And you'll find it within.
You need patience and persistence.
You need hope, and you need to keep
it close to the center of everything
that means the most to you.

You need to put things in perspective.
So much of your life lies ahead!
You need to know how good it can be.

You need to take the best of what
        you've learned from the old, and
        bring it to the beautiful days of
        a new journey.

Life's new beginnings happen for very
        special reasons.
When it's time to move on, remember
        that it really is okay.
Because when a new beginning unfolds
        in the story of your life, you go
        such a long way toward making the
        dreams of your tomorrows come true.

~ Douglas Pagels

If You Want Rainbows, You Gotta Have Rain

In a perfect world,
everything would always go right.
There would be no disappointments or trials,
and life would be filled with only
sweet, warm, and fuzzy feelings.

But how would we know
if things were good if we had no comparison?
Would we recognize the blessings in our lives
without having the opposite to compare them to?
Without the darkness,
would we appreciate the light?

Seems to me that if we want rainbows,
we gotta have rain.
The trick is to pull ourselves up by our bootstraps
and go out and look for puddles to play in;
recognize the tempest for what it is
and train ourselves to look for the good
in every situation.
By overcoming our adversity,
we find the joy in everything.
So go on, go play in the rain!

~ Suzy Toronto

The Path to Recovery

Recovery Is...
Breaking free, finding the strength, and having every ounce of faith it takes. It's earning and deserving a new beginning and facing the day with hope. It's being able to cope with anything that comes along, and staying healthy on every step of the journey.

The Journey Is...
A lifelong process that happens day by day. It's one that takes you away from guilt and pain. It's a path that will bring you closer to your loved ones and bring you so much joy and self-esteem. And it's one that leads to so much serenity.

Serenity Is...
The reward for having the determination
to make it work and working, step
by step, to get it right. It's relying on
strength and courage and all the support
you need to have a new and very special
life. God's gift to every one of us is
that we can mend and begin again and
never give up. Serenity is the sun that
follows the storm, and it's the warmth
of knowing how good life can be.

~ Douglas Pagels

Tomorrow Is a New Day

Sometimes we do not feel
   like we want to feel
Sometimes we do not achieve
   what we want to achieve
Sometimes things that happen
   do not make sense
Sometimes life leads us in directions
   that are beyond our control
It is at these times, most of all
that we need someone
who will quietly understand us
and be there to support us
I want you to know
that I am here for you
in every way
and remember that though
things may be difficult now
tomorrow is a new day

~ Susan Polis Schutz

When One Door Closes, Another One Opens

You are a very deserving person. And when someone like you has experienced a difficult time, there's a place you can count on to be there for you. That place is in the hearts of others... and in the comfort and care of every wish and every prayer.

As one door closes, you move on, but you do not journey alone. And in your time of need — another door does open, and it leads to a place where the days truly do get brighter and the load really does get lighter.

May you find peace in knowing that
somewhere up ahead, a brand-new door
is opening on a brand-new day...

And may your hopes for serenity
    and your prayers for guidance
        beautifully show you the way.

~ Alin Austin

Be Strong,
and Don't Give Up

Remember... there is a deeper strength
and an amazing abundance of peace
available to you.
Draw from this well;
call on your faith to uphold you.
You will make it through this time
and find joy in life again.

Life continues around us,
even when our troubles seem to stop time.
There is good in life every day.
Take a few minutes to distract yourself
from your concerns —
long enough to draw strength from a tree
or to find pleasure in a bird's song.

Return a smile;
realize that life is a series of levels,
cycles of ups and downs —
some easy, some challenging.
Through it all, we learn;
we grow strong in faith;
we mature in understanding.
The difficult times are often
the best teachers,
and there is good to be found
in all situations.
Reach for the good.

~ Pamela Owens Renfro

Resilience

I am driven by the beauty of a sunrise, an early-morning autumn breeze, a good cup of coffee.

I am driven by my inner strength and my desire to be what I have within me.

I am driven by hope and the poetry I know I can write.

I am driven by my husband's glistening eyes and my many silly nicknames and how he says I have a heart with an endless capacity for love.

I am driven by my puppy's head on my lap and the way she defies me unless I have treats.

I am driven by how we are all connected;
I am driven because we are the same.

I am driven by the beauty and generosity of
people who give kindness, understanding,
a wide smile, a helping hand.

I am driven to put away sorrow and fear and
return the favor, to celebrate the blessings
and to say thank you in this way, to mend
and to give that which is good to others.

I am driven to rediscover joy, to not give
up, to find me again.

~ Caroline Comerford

You Deserve a Medal for Your Strength and Courage

Sometimes you fight your way
through battle after battle
and show your strength and courage
by being a warrior.
You wait, listen to your heart,
find wisdom to take the right path,
and show your strength and courage
by being patient.
You stand up for what you believe in,
say "no" to that which is not
compatible with your values,
and show your strength and courage
by being true to yourself.

You open new doors for yourself
even when you seem too tired to go on.
You find the energy to see a new dawn —
a new point of view —
and create a new direction
where none seems possible.
You show your strength and courage
by being optimistic.
No matter how many times
you are knocked down,
you continue to rise again.
You deserve a medal to honor
your strength and courage.

~ Bonnie St. John

"When You Must, You Can"

It's just a few simple words, but this old saying contains one of the best reminders there is, and it is a wonderful thing to keep in mind. There have been times when I've found myself wondering... how am I going to make it through? What can I possibly do to remedy a certain problem? And how am I ever going to figure out what direction to go from here?

And then I remember those words: "When you must, you can."

That phrase has proven itself to be true in almost everything I've done. I have had days when I found strength inside me that I didn't even know I had. I have found answers to questions I thought I'd never solve.

I have surprised myself with my ability to
rise above certain situations and stay on top
of what it takes to find my serenity. At times
when I didn't think I could go on another day,
I reached deep and kept the faith and managed
to find a way.

I don't know how it works, but it does. Maybe,
through our belief, it's God's way of quietly
coming into our lives, walking by our side,
and giving us the help we need. Maybe it's
our guardian angels carrying us along until we
have the strength to stand on our own. Whatever
it is, it's a very reassuring thought. It's something
I plan on remembering as long as I live, and
I hope it will bring its beautiful blessing to you.

"When you must, you can." You can see your
way through.

~ Douglas Pagels

You Can Handle Any Problems That Life Brings

I know that lately you
have been having problems
and I just want you to know
that you can rely on me
  for anything
you might need
But more important
keep in mind at all times
that you are very capable
of dealing with any complications
that life has to offer
So
do whatever you must
feel whatever you must
and keep in mind at all times
that we all
grow wiser and
become more sensitive and
are able to enjoy life more
after we go through
hard times
                    ~ Susan Polis Schutz

At any given point in time,
there are hundreds of thoughts
moving through our minds.
Many times we worry
about a moment that has passed
or a day that has yet to come,
and many of us talk down to ourselves
for mistakes and misgivings,
leaving no room for forgiveness.

What we should realize
is that we, too, are human
and deserve the same
forgiveness and kindness
that we pass along to others.
So stop where you are
and change your negative thoughts.
Replace them with
something great about you.
You have so much going for you...
you just have to take a moment
to recognize it.

~ Lamisha Serf

Don't Forget to
Take Care of Yourself

Today, if only for a few moments, lay your burden aside and remember that there are people who care about you and are ready to help.

Set aside anger, worry, and endless tasks; be soothed by the love and kindness that surround you.

Do what integrity dictates, but take time to care for yourself. Be recharged and lifted in mind, body, and spirit.

Be kind to yourself, as you are to others, and accept the love and comfort that are offered.

Today, if only for a few moments, let your burdens be eased by someone else's strength.

~ Linda Sackett-Morrison

Listen to Your Heart and Trust Your Intuition

Your heart is listening and talking to you. It hears everything you say, knows everything you do, and feels everything you're feeling. It knows your secrets and regrets, faults and assets, weaknesses and strengths. It knows your family and the influences other people have had on you. It knows your habits and the state of your health. It knows your deepest desires and proudest moments. It wants to help you. It will make suggestions to you in a still, small voice that may come to you in unexpected ways, like something you just happen to hear or see or read. Sometimes you may want to ignore it because you think your mind will have better advice, but your heart will never steer you wrong.

Trust what you hear when your heart is talking to you. It holds your hopes and dreams. But it is not an inactive guardian or an idle keeper — it feels your hunger and understands your purpose in life. It knows what you need to do to fulfill that purpose — the changes you need to make and the methods that will assist you in making them. It will collect all the options unique to you to help you make the best choices for your life. Like a good friend, it will caution you and encourage you. It communicates with you through your intuition, and if you listen, it will help you find opportunities you never dreamed were possible. Practice listening to your heart, and don't be afraid to trust its guidance.

~ Donna Fargo

Believe in Your Power to Make Things Better

Sometimes it's hard to understand
how things can turn out so wrong
when your hopes were so high
and your intentions so good.
But life has a way of balancing
sorrow with joy,
disappointment with hope,
and emptiness with meaning.

You will look back on
the most painful experiences
as times of healing, growth,
and discovering your own strength.

You can see them as a challenge
to forgive the past and trust the future;
to feel the pain and move beyond it;
and to believe in life,
the hope of each tomorrow,
and the gift of every day.

Believe in yourself and in your power
to create your own best future —
to attract the things you need,
the people you love,
and all the joy you deserve.

~ Paula Finn

Grace Will Carry You

No matter where you have been,
no matter what you have done,
no matter how lost you may feel,
grace will carry you.

When the road of life becomes uncertain
and many questions seem to go unanswered,
look up and smile.

Receive each day's blessings with gladness,
for it is the twists and turns of life
that take you on a journey
you wouldn't have traveled otherwise.
All crossroads have a purpose.

One day you will look back and realize
that if it wasn't for the crossroad
with all its uncertainty,
you would never have made it
to where you were meant to be.

In that moment of arrival,
you will know that you were never alone.
You will know that your questions
were indeed answered with a voice
of compassion and love
that guided you safely home.

~ Lisa Mae Huddleston

Every night has its day. Every valley
has its mountaintop. Every problem
has a solution. Every down has its
up. Every frown has a smile to it. You
must be patient; wait and you will see.

Life is full of ups and downs —
mountains and valleys, smiles and
frowns. But friendship is there to
be found. Love is there to be found.
Bright moments are there to be
found... and therein lies the beauty.

~ Ashley Rice

Dreams can come true
if you take the time to
think about what you want in life...
Get to know yourself
Find out who you are
Choose your goals carefully
Be honest with yourself
But don't think about yourself so much
that you analyze every word and action
Don't become preoccupied with yourself
Find many interests and pursue them
Find out what is important to you
Find out what you are good at
Don't be afraid to make mistakes
Work hard to achieve successes
When things are not going right
don't give up — just try harder
Find courage inside of you to remain strong

Give yourself freedom to try out new things
Don't be so set in your ways that you can't grow
Always act in an ethical way
Laugh and have a good time
Form relationships with people you respect
Treat others as you want them to treat you
Be honest with people
Accept the truth
Speak the truth
Open yourself up to love
Don't be afraid to love
Remain close to your family
Take part in the beauty of nature
Be appreciative of all that you have
Help those less fortunate than you
Try to make other lives happy
Work toward peace in the world
Live life to the fullest

~ Susan Polis Schutz

You Will Win
This Battle!

You're strong like a beautiful tree in the forest.
You have experienced the winds of change
and challenge, and you are still standing. Like
the roots of a beautiful tree in the forest reach
down into the earth, your foundation of faith
and spirituality will keep you firmly planted.

When you've done all you think you can, stay
determined. When you're doubtful and frustrated,
don't give up. When you can't see tomorrow,
just get through today.

Keep on keeping on. You will win. Don't despair.
Storms and the weather made that big tree strong,
and it's still standing, too, just like you.

In the quiet of your heart and mind, you may
sometimes have questions. Stay positive, and
allow yourself to hope and dream, to rest and
relax. Believe that all things are possible, and
you will be empowered. Believe that you will
win this battle!

~ Donna Fargo

Keep These Bits
of Wisdom
Close to Your Heart

If a star twinkles... wish on it. When you spot a rainbow... search for the gold. Walk on the sunny side; dream on a cloud. Always remember that life is meant to be enjoyed.

Be gracious... angels are watching. Unfold your wings; rise and soar. Fill your life with wonder and your days with beauty. Set your dreams on the farthest star. When you're caught between a rock and a hard place... plant a seed. Chart your course; map out your future. Sail away on your own cruise line, and remember there's no limit to how far you can go.

Believe in miracles. Look for silver linings. When the going gets tough... let faith smooth the way.

Dreams come in all shapes and sizes. Do the things that warm your soul. Inspire yourself. Make good things happen. In every tomorrow a new promise shines.

Believe in yourself. Honor your strengths. A little hope and determination can overcome anything. Life is a candle... and you're its spark. Soar high and far. Open your arms, and let life's good things come in. God has some spectacular moments designed for you — and no one is more deserving than you.

Live your wishes. Blaze your own trail straight to the stars. Wherever you go... take a prayer with you. Follow your vision wherever it leads. Life is a gift and so are you. May wisdom, love, dreams, and angels walk with you always.

~ Linda E. Knight

Stay on Your Chosen Path

There are many paths to success.
Some are easy,
but those are very rare
and not without consequences.
Other paths are such a struggle —
a difficult climb all the way.

Sometimes the more you have to
fight for something,
the more it's worth it in the end.
Through that struggle,
you gain a greater sense of accomplishment
and a deeper feeling of satisfaction.

When you are facing struggles in your life,
you may look for another way out.
Stay your course.
Don't veer from your chosen path.

Remember... a struggle is just another
path to success.

~ Marion Wilson

Whenever two ways lie before us, one of which is easy and the other hard, one of which requires no exertion while the other calls for resolution and endurance, happy are those who choose the mountain path and scorn the thought of resting in the valley. These are the men and women who are destined in the end to conquer and succeed.

~ Author Unknown

Perhaps strength doesn't reside in
never having been broken, but in the
courage required to grow strong in
the broken places.

~ Author Unknown

Above the cloud with its shadow
is the star with its light.

~ Victor Hugo

Just Do Your Best

Sometimes you may
think that you
need to be perfect
that you cannot
make mistakes
At these times
you put so much
pressure on yourself
Try to realize
that you are
like everyone else —
capable of
reaching great potential
but not capable of
being perfect
Just do your best
and realize that
this is enough
Don't compare yourself
to anyone
Be happy to be
the wonderful
unique, very special
person that you are

~ Susan Polis Schutz

Take It One Day at a Time

You can do more than you think you can. Try to embrace the obstacles in your life as lessons and see every goal as reachable. Be patient. You'll dream new dreams in time. You'll find the keys that open the doors to your changing world.

For those mountains that don't seem to budge, you will find a way to move them. May your problems actually be opportunities in disguise. Every time your heart is broken, may you find a way to put it back together even stronger than ever. For those feelings of insecurity, may you get in touch with your power source inside you. Have hope. Have faith. Believe in miracles.

May your disappointments turn into steppingstones.
May these new circumstances transcribe the
writing on the wall into positive actions you
can take. As you deal with your loneliness and
examine all your wishes that may be hiding in
your heart... may you have an angel to walk
beside you, friends who will always be there,
and answers to every prayer that you pray.

Find a mantra to say over and over when you're
discouraged, like... "I am strong, and the best
is yet to come."

~ Donna Fargo

Angels Are Watching Over You

There are angels among us.
You may have encountered
   one lately.
It may have been someone
who offered an encouraging word,
   a helping hand,
      or a simple smile.
Angels know how to touch
   through human hands
      and love through human hearts.
It doesn't take a miracle to recognize
   when an angel has been at work.
Just open your eyes
   and watch for love in action.

Angels are everywhere.
Seen or unseen, they lift spirits,
    encourage the downhearted,
        and offer heavenly help
            for down-to-earth problems.

If you hear the sound of wings, remember:
    angels are watching over you.

~ Candy Paull

Keep Faith Beside You

When all else fades and melts away, faith remains. Like a flower that blossoms in the midst of a storm, your faith will grow and bloom when you least expect it.

When you feel you've prayed every prayer and wished every wish, faith will knock gently and ask to be let in. Choose faith and you choose life. Choose faith and you choose courage. Choose faith and you choose to follow the urgings of your spirit, no matter what hardships are tearing at your heart.

There is no test to prove yourself worthy of faith. Simply invite her in, and you'll feel the arms of faith wrap around you and embrace you with quiet comfort. You'll rest in the knowing that faith is an unspoken prayer that will never leave your side.

If you have but one wish, let it be that faith stays with you always. For with faith beside you, you will never be alone.

~ Rachel Snyder

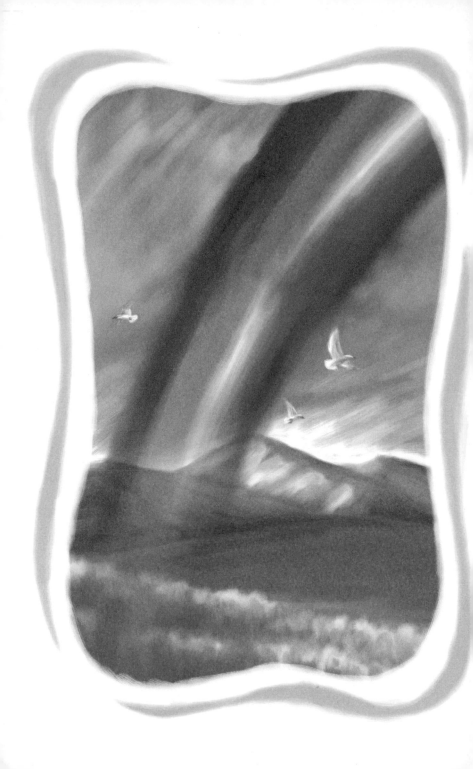

The Sun Will Shine Again

When we are in the midst of a storm,
sometimes it's hard to believe
the sun is waiting to shine again.
But God's love is just like the sun —
even when you cannot see it
it is waiting to fill your days
and your heart with warmth and light.

Trust that every hard time ends,
that prayers are answered —
sometimes quickly,
   sometimes slowly —
and that rainbows follow the rain.

You will come through this challenge,
and when you look back,
you will see it has made you stronger
and given you gifts
   you never imagined.

                  ~ Jason Blume

Happiness Is a Choice Within Us All

Many people believe that happiness is a place you get to after years of dreaming and thinking "If only..."

Some people believe that happiness equals the money in the bank, the car in their driveway, or the clothes on their back.

Others know that happiness isn't a place or an item that can be seen and felt. They know it is a way of living and an attitude of being.

Happiness is a choice.

Every day that we wake, we have an opportunity to bring happiness to ourselves and others simply by making a choice to do so.

Even in desperate times, in times of sorrow and fear, we have the choice to look on the bright side of every event that comes our way.

If you can take a moment and think of what makes you happy, you will find that happiness isn't in things — it's simply within us all. We all have the ability to experience happiness, no matter what life throws at us. We just have to make the choice.

~ Lamisha Serf

So Many People Care About You

You may think you are
alone at the moment,
and you may feel as if
you are just soldiering on.
But you couldn't be more wrong,
because you have a whole army
of people behind you.

So the next time you feel alone
    with your problems
or feel downhearted in any way,
remember that army of supporters
    behind you —
people who care about you
    and are wishing you well.
May this thought make you feel
    a whole lot better
and help to keep you strong.

~ Maria Mullins

Wherever You Go, Leave Good Footprints

Life is a precious journey we all take. Each decision we make leaves an indelible footprint, for good or bad, success or failure, happiness or sorrow. So walk carefully and with much thought, for your footprints will follow you wherever you go.

Make good footprints. Walk in love. Reach out in kindness. Speak peace. Harm no one. Be a light for goodness. Live in truth. Spread hope. Embrace others. Build bridges. Be a friend to all. Show compassion. Champion respect. Give your best. Do what is right. Make a difference. (Everyone can!)

Live your life in such a thoughtful and honorable way that when you or others look back on the landscape of your life, you will feel proud of the footprints you have left behind.

Good footprints will not only allow you to live well, happy, and at peace. They will make this world — which sometimes seems so crazy — a better place because it was graced by your presence, blessed by your spirit, and gifted by the bright legacy you left.

Wherever you go in this life... leave good footprints behind you.

~ Nancye Sims

Bless the Challenges
You've Weathered

Every rock in the road...
bless it.
Every pain, every struggle...
forgive it.
Every tear shed, every mournful wail,
every storm that's knocked you down...
bless them all.

Thank your body for waking you up,
for healing.

Be grateful to your heart
for leading you to greater love.

Honor your courage
to heed the call to grow.

Hard as it has been,
every challenge has strengthened your will
and enlivened your spirit.

Bless them all...
and you will be blessed.

~ Rachel Snyder

Always Hope for the Best

Don't let go of hope.
Hope gives you the strength to keep going
when you feel like giving up.
Don't ever quit believing in yourself.
As long as you believe you can,
you will have a reason for trying.
Don't let anyone hold your happiness
in their hands; hold it in yours,
so it will always be within your reach.
Don't measure success or failure
by material wealth
but by how you feel;
our feelings determine
the richness of our lives.
Don't let bad moments overcome you;
be patient, and they will pass.
Don't hesitate to reach out for help;
we all need it from time to time.

Don't run away from love but toward love,
because it is our deepest joy.
Don't wait for what you want
to come to you.
Go after it with all that you are,
knowing that life will meet you halfway.
Don't feel like you've lost
when plans and dreams
fall short of your hopes.
Anytime you learn something new
about yourself or about life,
you have progressed.
Don't do anything that takes away
from your self-respect.
Feeling good about yourself
is essential to feeling good about life.
Don't ever forget how to laugh
or be too proud to cry.
It is by doing both
that we live life to its fullest.

~ Nancye Sims

These Words Will Help You Get Through Just About Anything

Stay positive! (Hopeful people are happier people.) ⤳ Choose wisely. (Good choices will come back to bless you.) ⤳ Remember what matters. (The present moment. The good people in it. Hopes and dreams and feelings.)

⤳ Don't stress out over things you can't control. (Just don't.) ⤳ Count every blessing. (Even the little ones add up to a lot.) ⤳ Be good to your body. (It's the only one you get.)

⌒ Listen to the wishes of your heart. (It always seems to know what's true, what's right, what to do, and where to go with your life.)

⌒ Understand how special you are! ⌒ Realize how strong you can be. ⌒ And know that, YES, you're going to make it through, no matter what.

Maybe you won't be dancing in the streets or jumping on the bed... but you are going to get through the day, the night, and each and every moment that lies ahead. (I promise.)

～ Douglas Pagels

Everything Is Going
to Work Out

Remember: things do work out.
Storms pass. Hearts mend.
Memories heal.
And as each day rises
new and fresh, so too
will new dreams and purpose
find their way to you.

Be still. Stand strong. Stay steady.
New beginnings filled with purpose
are just ahead of you.
Embrace the little things that comfort you —
the love of family, the hand of friendship,
the prayers of all.
May everything you hold dear
come back to you.

May strong words of hope
give you courage.
Know beyond a doubt
that you already have
all the faith you need.
There are so many treasures
yet to be found
and so many tomorrows
waiting for you.
Push on to what lies ahead,
and let love clear the way.
You are such a very special soul,
and you will get through this.

~ Linda E. Knight

"Hang In There"

Difficulties arise in the lives of us all. What is most important is dealing with the hard times, coping with the changes, and getting through to the other side where the sun is still shining just for you.

It takes a strong person to deal with tough times and difficult choices. But you are a strong person. It takes courage. But you possess the inner courage to see you through. It takes being an active participant in your life. But you are in the driver's seat, and you can determine the direction you want tomorrow to go in.

Hang in there... and take care to see that you don't lose sight of the one thing that is constant, beautiful, and true: everything will be fine — and it will turn out that way because of the special kind of person you are.

So... beginning today and lasting a lifetime through... hang in there, and don't be afraid to feel like the morning sun is shining... just for you.

~ Douglas Pagels

ACKNOWLEDGMENTS

We gratefully acknowledge the permission granted by the following authors, publishers, and authors' representatives to reprint poems or excerpts from their publications.

PrimaDonna Entertainment Corp. for "Life Hurts Sometimes," "Listen to Your Heart and Trust Your Intuition," "Ten Golden Rules for a Better Life," "You Will Win This Battle!" and "Take It One Day at a Time" by Donna Fargo. Copyright © 2005, 2006, 2007, 2008, 2012 by PrimaDonna Entertainment Corp. All rights reserved.

Jason Blume for "They Say Hard Times Make Us Stronger," "Courage is not the absence of fear…," and "The Sun Will Shine Again." Copyright © 2007, 2012 by Jason Blume. All rights reserved.

Julie Rojics for "You Can Accomplish Anything You Put Your Mind To." Copyright © 2012 by Julie Rojics. All rights reserved.

Suzy Toronto for "If You Want Rainbows, You Gotta Have Rain." Copyright © 2008 by Suzy Toronto. All rights reserved.

Caroline Comerford for "Resilience." Copyright © 2012 by Caroline Comerford. All rights reserved.

Lamisha Serf for "At any given point in time…" and "Happiness Is a Choice Within Us All." Copyright © 2012 by Lamisha Serf. All rights reserved.

Linda Sackett-Morrison for "Don't Forget to Take Care of Yourself." Copyright © 2012 by Linda Sackett-Morrison. All rights reserved.

Paula Finn for "Believe in Your Power to Make Things Better." Copyright © 2012 by Paula Finn. All rights reserved.

Lisa Mae Huddleston for "Grace Will Carry You." Copyright © 2012 by Lisa Mae Huddleston. All rights reserved.

Linda E. Knight for "Keep These Bits of Wisdom Close to Your Heart" and "Everything Is Going to Work Out." Copyright © 2012 by Linda E. Knight. All rights reserved.

Marion Wilson for "Stay on Your Chosen Path." Copyright © 2012 by Marion Wilson. All rights reserved.

Candy Paull for "Angels Are Watching Over You." Copyright © 2012 by Candy Paull. All rights reserved.

Rachel Snyder for "Keep Faith Beside You" and "Bless the Challenges You've Weathered." Copyright © 2012 by Rachel Snyder. All rights reserved.

Nancye Sims for "Wherever You Go, Leave Good Footprints." Copyright © 2012 by Nancye Sims. All rights reserved.

A careful effort has been made to trace the ownership of selections used in this anthology in order to obtain permission to reprint copyrighted material and give proper credit to the copyright owners. If any error or omission has occurred, it is completely inadvertent, and we would like to make corrections in future editions provided that written notification is made to the publisher:

BLUE MOUNTAIN ARTS, INC., P.O. Box 4549, Boulder, Colorado 80306.